The Skills of Appraisal

Peter Packard and John Slater

A Gower Audio Manual

Published by
Gower Publishing Company Limited,
Gower House,
Croft Road,
Aldershot
Hants GU11 3HR,
England

Gower Publishing Company,
Old Post Road,
Brookfield,
Vermont 05036,
USA

British Library Cataloguing in Publication Data
Packard, Peter
   The skills of appraisal.
   1. Employees, Rating of
   I. Title   II. Slater, John
   658.3'125   HF5549.5.R3

Library of Congress Cataloging-in-Publication Data
Slater, John
   The skills of appraisal/John Slater and Peter Packard. p.   cm.
   Bibliography: p.
   1. Employees, Rating of. 2. Performance standards.
3. Interviewing.   I. Packard, Peter. II. Title.
HF5549.5.R3S57 1988
658.3'125—dc19   87–22388
                  CIP

ISBN 0–566–02729–1

Contents

Introduction

To be effective, appraisal interviewing requires a high level of skill. Such skill can be acquired only by practice, coupled with the ability to be self-analytical.

It is important to emphasize that there is no one 'right way' to conduct an interview since any interaction between two human beings has an infinite number of variables. The 'right way' is the way that works for that appraiser with that subject at that particular time.

There are, however, certain principles in appraisal which an individual can use to formulate his or her approach. These can then be adapted by the appraiser to suit his particular style and the circumstances of a particular interview. It is to these principles that this package is addressed.

Who is it for?

This package is designed for those who have to appraise the performance of others and wish to improve their skills. It is equally suitable for experienced managers and supervisors and for those who are appraising for the first time. It is not intended to be a substitute for formal training but is complementary to the training process.

Objectives

The package will help appraisers to focus upon the process of the appraisal interview and in particular the need for skill in:

- Structuring the interview
- Obtaining information in an objective way
- Use of appropriate management style
- Diagnosing the next steps necessary to improve performance
- Gaining commitment to future action and objectives.

Method

The tape and text are designed as a self-teaching package. The tape is used to show examples of good and bad interviewing technique, particularly in opening the interview, strategy and questioning techniques to obtain information, and closing the interview.

Part I

The Appraisal Process

1   The purpose of appraisal

It is most important that there is a shared understanding of the purpose for which appraisal and its supporting system are designed. Many employees look upon appraisal as an occasion when their boss 'tells' them how they have done; some see it as an integral part of the salary system, whilst to others it is an objective-setting exercise. Unless both managers and employees fully understand its purpose the true potential of appraisal may not be realized. There may even be a negative outcome.

Exercise

Each organization has specific purposes for which it requires appraisal to be carried out. Write below the specific purpose(s) of *your* organization's appraisal system:

Performance appraisal has two purposes:

1   Providing a means for managers to improve the performance of their groups by way of individual support and guidance.
2   Obtaining and sharing information. From this may come:
    -   plans for meeting needs in the present job
    -   decisions on salary
    -   career planning.

The first purpose is all too often neglected: it is hard to do, but not hard to avoid. It is very easy to rely on the system alone and neglect the skill needed to make it work. If the appraisal system is directed towards improving the performance of the individual it will improve the organization as a whole.

This is why the appraisal interview is crucial to the system. Constructive discussion about how subordinates are going about their jobs can be helpful to them and revealing to the manager. It can bring out information on which to base actions which will help the subordinate continue to do a good job, or to improve. People learn naturally; appraisal is a means of speeding up learning.

Used in this way – a skill-driven approach – appraisal becomes an active and constructive pursuit. A passive 'reporting' of past events occurs when a systems-driven approach is adopted and employees have no chance to learn how they can improve or develop.

The next chapter describes how an appraisal system can be made active by directing it towards improving the performance of the individual through constructive discussion.

2 Active appraisal – the skills approach

The skills approach concentrates upon:

- Development rather than evaluation
- Behavioural as well as quantitative objectives
- The future as well as the past
- A problem-solving as well as a tell–sell style (see Appendix 1).

To clarify the approach the essential components can be further broken down into *development steps* and *motivation growth*.

Development steps increase the *capacity* of the subject:

(a)   to do his/her present job, based upon recent performance.
(b)   to meet anticipated changes in content of the present job.
(c)   to contribute to career growth.

Motivation growth means increasing the *inclination* of the subject to do the job now and in the near future.

The crucial aspect of performance improvement is to diagnose what needs to be improved *next* to add to the capacity of an individual.

Similarly, what is the *next* thing to do to add to the inclination of an individual to work, i.e to achieve motivation growth?

3　The appraisal process

To achieve these development steps and motivation growth we need to examine the appraisal process as shown in Figure 1.

Firstly we cannot work without *information*, which must be shared – is what we *believe* to be true *really* true?

Next we must *diagnose* the *next step* necessary to increase *capacity* and/or *inclination*.

Then we must *show and gain commitment*. Commitment cannot be demanded, it must be earned. It is much more likely to be earned if appraisees are encouraged to make the diagnosis and suggest the treatment themselves.

Next we need clear, definite *action* – as distinct from intention.

Lastly we must *report* to the organization and finally *monitor* to see that action takes place.

We can now examine what this means in practice.

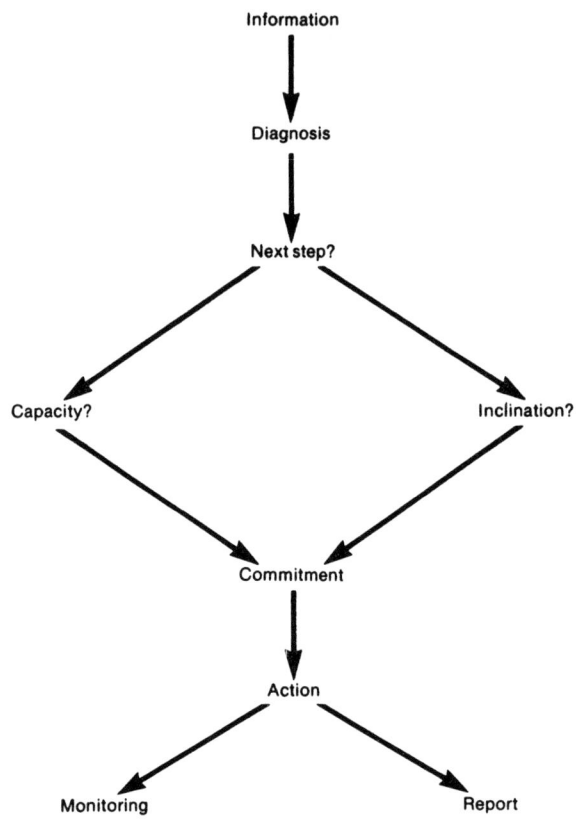

Fig. 1 The appraisal interview process

4   The nature of appraisal skill

Appraisal skill is complex. In this manual we can only make a start on developing the skill by outlining the principles and developing the facility for analysis. Skill can only be developed by self-analysis and awareness of the process of the interaction.

It means being careful about the things you do. You must look at the interview as though you are watching someone else do it, and learn from this. You will also need to show that positive and helpful things happen when the subordinate talks frankly.

Here are some ground rules towards growing more skilful:

1   Remember all the time why you are there. For instance, if you remember why you are there it will be clear that you raise 'critical' incidents to elicit more information, not to admonish the appraisee.
2   Be exact in using praise. That is, relate praise to the actual things that were done well, rather than giving it vaguely and indiscriminately. It is not a bad idea to start with praise. People expect it when they have earned it, so why not start with it? Hearing the good news first and therefore knowing where you stand makes you more receptive to the bad news later.
3   Use questions effectively. Use:

OPEN questions to open up topics.
PROBES to get the detail, reasons, perceptions, etc.
CLOSED questions to establish specific facts.
REFLECTIVES to promote the flow of information, to stay with a specific point.

and be wary of using:
Leading questions – they have an inbuilt answer.
Multiple questions – they are confusing.
Hypothetical questions – they produce hypothetical answers.

You will be hearing some examples of different ways of asking and phrasing questions later in the tape. See also the table on page 53.

4 Wherever possible ask questions and invite comments in a value-free way. Note the difference in the *quality* and tone of information which you would expect in response to:

'You lost Smith last year – I think that you handled that matter rather badly.'

and

'You lost Smith last year – tell me about that.'

5 Research into appraisal shows that in many cases appraisees are left in the dark about what the boss thinks of them. Bear in mind that most appraisees look forward to hearing what the appraiser thinks of their work. Also, appraisees are not usually so much interested in what 'the organization' thinks as in what their immediate boss thinks.

6 Help the appraisees arrive at their own conclusions and deductions, or summarize those that they have arrived at, to them. That is, help them see for themselves, rather than tell them.

7 Check that you are not talking too much yourself. In appraisal the appraiser should learn things as well as the appraisee. As a general rule, when we are talking we are not learning much.

There are other factors that contribute to the success of an interview.

1 Choose the right style – there is no one best style, though everyone has a style in which they feel most at ease. A range of styles exists and the thoughtful manager chooses the best one for each circumstance.

The authoritarian style has been much criticized, although it is not a 'bad' style in itself: we all need to be told what to do at times. However, if it is used inappropriately during an appraisal:

- appraisees may not bring out useful ideas;
- they may not feel committed to what the appraiser is telling them;

- there is a greater chance that the manager will take a biased or one sided view;
- there is a greatly reduced chance of either party learning anything.

See also Appendix 1.

2   Use evidence – appraisal works best when it is based on evidence rather than assertion. On the tape you will hear the effect of assertion. It also works best when evidence is shared with the subordinate and compared with the appraisee's views.

   This is why we advise the use of 'critical incidents' as points for discussion when talking about performance. It is important that the subject is made aware that such 'incidents' are raised to learn from them, not to admonish him or her, or only to praise good work.

3   Concentrate on behaviour – not attitude – attitude is subjective; behaviour need not be. Appraisers who concentrate on the appraisee's attitude are being subjective.

   We can only guess about attitude, but we can see behaviour and its effects. Appraisers who concentrate upon behaviour are being objective. They are less likely to become involved in arguments, and find less need to explain and justify their comments, than those who make assertions about attitude.

4   Try to ensure actions – rather than intentions. Actions are clear and specific; intentions are vague and general. It is all too easy to allow the appraisee to close a topic by promising 'to look into it some time'.

5   Aim for commitment. Commitment implies some form of inner motivation or understanding requiring no pressure from the manager to ensure desirable action.

   If managers apply pressure they will nearly always achieve compliance. This is wasteful; it means that managers must watch subordinates to make sure they do as they are told, thus using time or energy which could be used on more creative or useful things.

Exercise

Re-phrase the following as open or value-free questions.

1   'Was it time pressure or cost that governed your decision?'

2   'I assume you checked it out fully with Administration?'

3   'Couldn't you have been more tactful?'

4   'I suppose you did it that way because . . .'

5   'I've had a bad time from Marketing over your failure to. . .'

6   'I don't think it was very wise to tell Smith.'

Some guidelines are given on the next page.

Notes

1   Effect: The appraisee is forced into selecting time or cost – but there may be some other reason. The question could be rephrased as 'What factors governed your decision?'

2   Effect: The interviewer wants the answer 'yes' so the appraisee will probably give it. If the question were rephrased: 'To what extent did you check it out with Administration?' it would be more likely to produce useful information.

3   Effect: The appraisee will probably agree but he may not know *how* to be more tactful. 'Can you think of a different approach you might have used?' would help him or her to think it through.

4   Effect: The appraiser will be given the answer 'yes'. 'Why did you choose to do it that way?' would elicit more information as to how the appraisee's mind was working.

5   Effect: The interviewer has indicated the consequences so the appraisee will be forced onto the defensive. 'Tell me what happened when . . .' is value-free.

6   Effect: The interviewer has revealed his values so again the appraisee will need to defend his or her actions. 'How did Smith come to know about it?' would produce the true facts.

Summary

We have been emphasizing the need to make appraisal purposeful and objective.

By concentrating on an active approach we are aiming to help individuals become better at their jobs. So we are improving the organization and, at the same time, helping employees attain their full potential.

We have been emphasizing the need to be skilful:

- in using hard evidence so that we can make better decisions;
- in selecting the appropriate style for the situations;
- in diagnosing the next steps to take; and
- in gaining the commitment of the appraisees rather than their compliance.

Part II

The Appraisal Interview

Introduction

Any purposeful discussion between two or more people is likely to be more successful if it is structured. Unstructured discussions are useful when creativity is required but for business purposes they are usually unsatisfactory and unproductive.

If we examine the ingredients of a successful meeting we find firstly that the purpose is clearly defined and there is a published agenda. The chairman introduces each item and ensures that discussion is to the point and that each participant can make his or her contribution fully and freely. He or she summarizes and clarifies action before moving on to the next point.

An appraisal interview is in fact a business meeting between two people with the express purpose of helping the appraisee become more effective. Thus a structure will go a long way towards helping both participants achieve this aim.

The framework is shown in Figure 2. It consists of three components – the opening, which sets the scene, the context and content; the middle, which contains a number of agenda items; the ending, which checks and restates the actions agreed. The time dimension cannot be quantified and is 'as long as is necessary to achieve the objective'.

We shall consider each component separately in the following chapters.

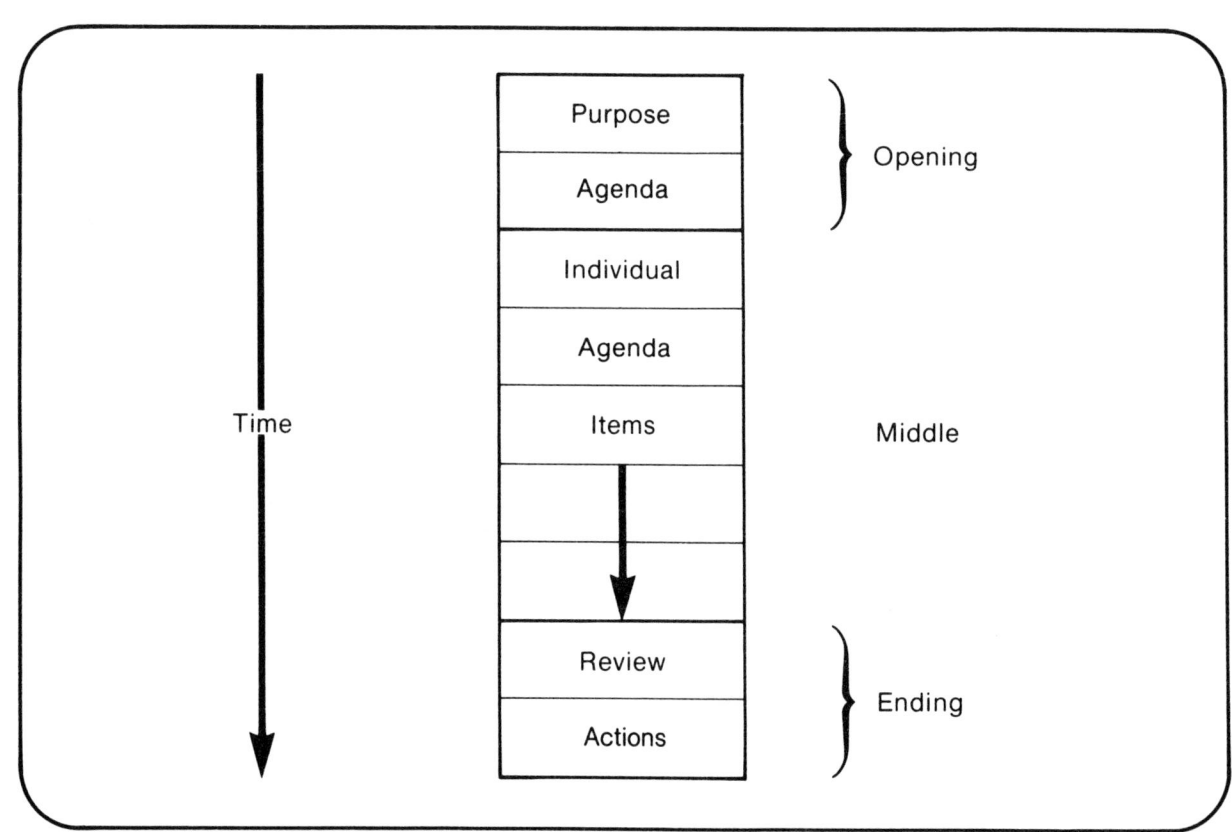

Fig. 2 The framework of an appraisal interview

The taped case study

John Benham is Production Manager of a manufacturing unit, one of three in Standard Pharmaceuticals plc. Like many managers in industry he has his share of domestic as well as business pressures. At work he is struggling hard to meet his objectives, whilst at home the expenses of maintaining a family are growing.

John is very concerned about his future. He has had five years in his present job and feels ready for more responsibility. He has delegated quite a lot of his work to his deputy in order to maintain his motivation. He is becoming concerned about what his next move is. It is known that the Production Manager of the Southampton unit, a much bigger plant, will be retiring shortly. John could do with this job and particularly the higher salary that goes with it. He is looking forward to his appraisal interview with his boss, Harold Mitchell. It will be a chance to air a number of problems that he is meeting and, more important, to raise the question of his future.

Harold Mitchell is the company's Production Director. Fundamentally he is a good manager; he keeps his ear to the ground and knows pretty well what goes on in his three production plants. There are two items he wants to investigate at John's appraisal interview. Firstly, John achieved most of last year's objectives but ran into problems over stock levels. The Marketing Manager, Peter Jarvis, has complained that customers had to wait ten days for a particular product while supplies were produced. He has taken this complaint to Board level and made things uncomfortable for Harold.

There are rumours that John has become a little unpopular lately with his supervisors. He is driving them hard and taking decisions which he would normally have left to them. This is unlike John and Harold needs to find out what is at the bottom of it.

5 Preparation

Harold has sent for John for his appraisal. John enters Harold's office, where Harold is on the telephone.

 *Start the tape*

Harold   *(on telephone)* There's no point in beating about the bush, you're either going to bring it back on target or you're not; and it had better be the former. I've got enough production problems this end without you adding to them. . . . Yes, let me know as soon as possible. Ah, John . . . right . . . now where was I? . . . Yes, your appraisal.

Would you like some coffee? *(he phones)* . . . Coffee for two, please, June . . . Two sugars, isn't it, John? . . . Yes, two sugars. Thanks.

Now it seems you've got a few problems, John.

John   Problems?

Harold   Yes, for example . . . *(door opens)* Ah, thank you, June. . . .

Now this out-of-stock situation. Peter Jarvis has already brought it up in front of the Board and that sort of pressure I can do without, so for goodness' sake make sure it doesn't happen again.

John   Hang on, Harold, that's not exactly fair; after all, it was caused by late orders and we turned the situation round in record time. What do they want? Blood?

Harold   I'm not concerned as to why it happened, I just don't want it repeated, OK? Just remember Peter and the MD are old friends – I can't fight that. So get yourself organized.

John   But it was only ten days.

Harold   Ten days, two days, I don't care if it was one day! Fix it!

(Phone rings)

John	But it's not as simple as that; you wanted cost kept to a minimum and I can't do both . . .
Harold	*(answering phone)* Yes, Don . . . good, have you got a completion date? . . . Oh come on, that's no good at all. . . . I don't care what the contractors say, that line is going back on stream on the date agreed. . . . OK, if you can't handle it I'll have to do it myself. *(to John)* Look, John, I'm going to have to sort this out, so we'll have to finish; was there anything important you wanted to talk about?
John	Well . . . er . . . er . . . not really.
Harold	Come on, come on.
John	No, forget it, it doesn't really matter.
Harold	OK. Keep up the good work, and for Heaven's sake don't give Peter another chance to complain . . . JUNE!

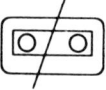 *Stop the tape. Now carry out the following exercise.*

Exercise

No interview could be as bad as this! However, it embodies many of the faults that people have been guilty of in the past. List those you identified. (Suggestions appear on the next page.)

Notes

1 Harold wasn't prepared.
2 He had not set up the right environment e.g. interruptions – coffee, telephone
3 There was no sign of any shared understanding of the purpose of the interview.
4 John couldn't even begin to raise the question of his future.

In fact, Harold should never have even started the interview as it has merely made matters worse.

It is most important for the appraiser to prepare himself properly – after all, this is a highly important event for both appraiser and appraisee.

Here is a checklist for preparation.

- Check appraisee's job description – any changes?
- Check last year's appraisal/objectives.
- What points do you want to discuss? – critical incidents? – evidence?
- What will he/she want to discuss – likely problems?
- Any delicate areas? – what questions will best open them up?
- What new objectives would you like to set?
- Have you set sufficient time aside?
- Will you be free of interruptions? – your office or elsewhere?
- How are you both going to sit? Remember your desk represents a barrier and a symbol of your authority – do you want this?
- Have you warned your secretary/switchboard not to pass on telephone calls?
- WHAT IS THE PURPOSE OF THE INTERVIEW?

Finally, remember that things do not always turn out as planned. Fresh information could emerge during the interview which may mean changing your mind.

6 The opening

Openings may take only five or ten minutes but they are crucial to the success of the interview.

In Figure 3 (overleaf) we show the two components of the opening. First of all it is important to clarify the *purpose* of the interview. The appraiser's mind may be clear, but is the appraisee really aware that the object is to help him or her to perform better? A re-statement emphasizes your interest in achieving a successful outcome.

Next, an *agenda* can be built up; the appraiser needs to know what, in particular, the appraisee wants to talk about. At the same time the appraiser needs to signal what points are on his own agenda. The skill arises in deciding and agreeing the order. Is a particular item of such importance to the appraisee that it should be dealt with first? If it is placed lower down the list, will he or she be in a receptive state of mind to discuss other matters rationally?

The process of agenda-building is a useful means of gauging how appraisees are feeling and what their priorities and concerns seem to be.

 *Start the tape*

Narrator	Imagine that the last scene never happened and that Harold has the chance to start again.
Harold	*(on phone)* John, I've finished what I had to do. If you're free, perhaps we could have a chat now. . . . OK. See you in a minute. *(to secretary)* Thank you, June, that's all for the moment. Now I've got John Benham coming in for his appraisal; so no interruptions and, please, no phone calls. Would you ask him to come in as soon as he arrives, and bring us a couple of cups of coffee? Thanks.

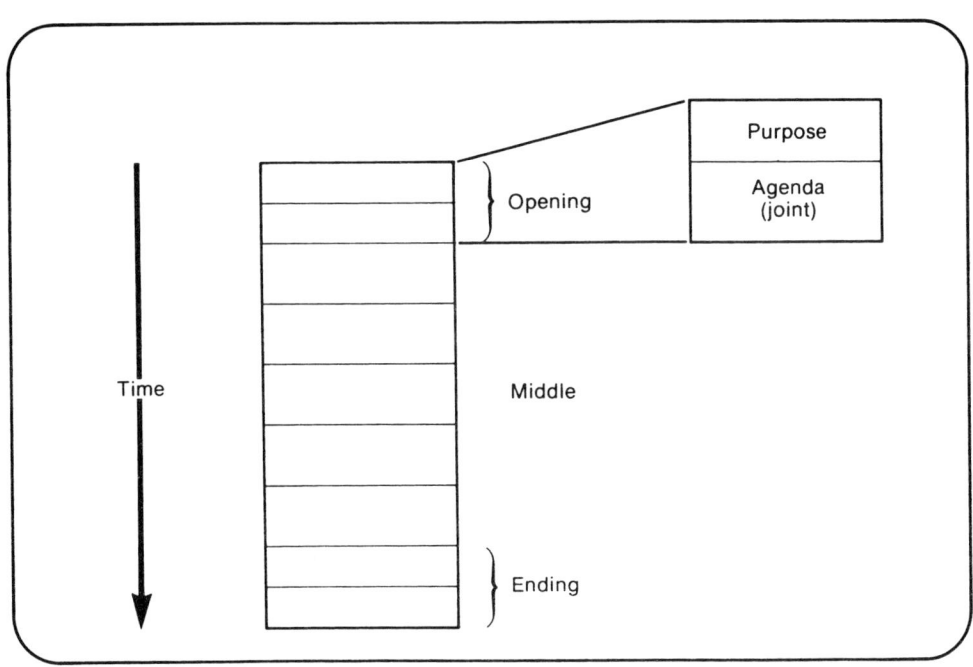

Fig. 3   The questioning process

(Door opens)

Ah, hello, John, pull up a chair. . . Thanks, June.

Mmm . . . yes . . . mmm. Well, John, as you know, it's appraisal time: the whole object being to tell you how you've performed over the year. I've got it all written down here so there shouldn't be anything much to add; after all, we see each other every day. But if you have something to say, please feel free to speak your mind.

John	Well, actually, Harold, there are one or two things – I'd like to iron out this stock level question, but more importantly. . . .
Harold	Well, let's take the stock level problem first. Now we both recognize it as a problem . . .
John	Yes, Harold, but . . .
Harold	Now I've had Peter Jarvis from Marketing on my back about your late deliveries of Sundown . . .
John	Oh no, not that one . . .
Narrator	Harold has forgotten the purpose and has started to *tell* him rather than *help* him. Let's listen to it again. . . .
Harold	Ah, hello, John, pull up a chair . . . Thanks, June. Mmm . . . yes . . . mmm. Well, John, as you know it's appraisal time; the whole object being to tell you how you've performed over the year. I've got it all written down here. . .
Narrator	Let's stop for a moment. It is really to *tell* him? It might be more help to both of them to check John's side of things to make sure that Harold has all the facts. Also, he said he has already got it written down, so it's unlikely that he'll find it easy to change his mind. Let's allow him to carry on.

Harold	. . . so there shouldn't be anything much to add. After all, we see each other every day. But if you have something to say, please feel free to speak your mind.
John	Well, actually, Harold, there are one or two things – I'd like to iron out this stock level question, but more importantly. . .
Harold	Well, let's take the stock level problem first. Now we both recognize it as a problem . . .
John	Yes, Harold, but . . .
Harold	Now I've had Peter Jarvis from Marketing on my back about your. . .

| Narrator | Twice John indicated that there was something important he wanted to talk about and twice Harold interrupted him as he was anxious to start on his own agenda.

John is exasperated because what is important to *him* is his future and here he is having to go over old ground. He is unlikely to respond positively.

In the next scene we can hear how it might have been done better. |

| Harold | Thank you, June, that's all for the moment.

Now, I've got John Benham coming in for his appraisal, so no interruptions and, please, no phone calls. Would you ask him to come in as soon as he arrives, and bring us a couple of cups of coffee? Thanks.

(pause)

John, let's sit over here. Coffee's on the way. Right, before I go any further I'd like to say one thing. The company has had a good year this year and I really appreciate your contribution over the last twelve months; your reaction to the stock cost problem was first class, and on the whole production targets have been met on time and within budget . . . so . . . Thanks.

Now, I know we've done it before, but let's just remind ourselves of what we are trying to do. . . .

Ah, thanks, June. . .

Right, let's do what we usually do. We'll discuss any of the things that are of concern to you, review the objectives we agreed last time and your performance, and then use |

	that to build next year's objectives and improvements . . . and, lastly, we've got to set down on paper what we've agreed.

that to build next year's objectives and improvements . . . and, lastly, we've got to set down on paper what we've agreed.

So, John, it's your day, what do you want to talk about?

John   Yes, well, . . . there are a few things – look, I'd like to iron out this problem I've had with Marketing over the stock levels of Sundown and sort out exactly what you'd like me to do. Also, it looks as though we've got some manning problems coming up on the new line, and if I don't get a decision soon it could delay the start-up.

But, Harold . . . what I *really* want to talk about is my future.

Harold   Your future?

John   Yes . . . Look, I've done five years in the job and frankly I think that I'm ready to take on more responsibility.

Remember, we agreed last year that I should give more responsibility to George so that he could take over. Well, if he doesn't move up soon he'll get demotivated and I reckon we could lose him.

Harold   OK, John, you want to talk about stock levels, they're on my list too. Also the manning problems on the new line, but particularly you want to talk about your future. One other thing I'd like to add to the list is to hear what your thoughts are about your supervisors.

So, can we get the present out of the way first and then we can concentrate on the future?

John   Fine . . .

Harold   Stock levels were top of your list, so let's start with those. . .

Narrator   This time Harold's done a lot better; he immediately relaxed John and made him more receptive by picking out some good points of his performance first; he set the scene, wisely asking John what he wanted to talk about so he could see how the land lay before adding any subjects of his own. Even more important, he was listening; let's hear again how he used a reflective question to encourage John to expand on the subject of his future.

John	. . . and if I don't get a decision soon it could delay the start-up.
	But, Harold. . . what I *really* want to talk about is my future.
Harold	Your future?
John	Yes . . . Look, I've done five years in the job and frankly I think that I'm ready to take on more responsibility.
	Remember, we agreed last year that I should give more responsibility. . .

Narrator   Harold realizes how important the question of John's future is but he needs to know how strong his feeling are. A reflective question is an ideal way of obtaining more information.

We have now heard three openings. The last one, although not perfect, goes a long way to providing the good start that is so necessary. He got the atmosphere right. He checked the purpose. He built a joint agenda. The way he did that allowed him to find out John's primary concern – his future. He signalled clearly to John that this point had registered with him.

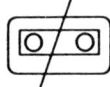

Stop the tape and return to the text

You have now heard three examples of beginnings. The last example differed significantly from the first two in that it *clarified the purpose of the interview* and *agreed an agenda between the participants*. By doing this, Harold has achieved the two main objectives of a beginning.

7   The middle

All the main work is done in the middle – gathering information – comparing views – arriving at actions.

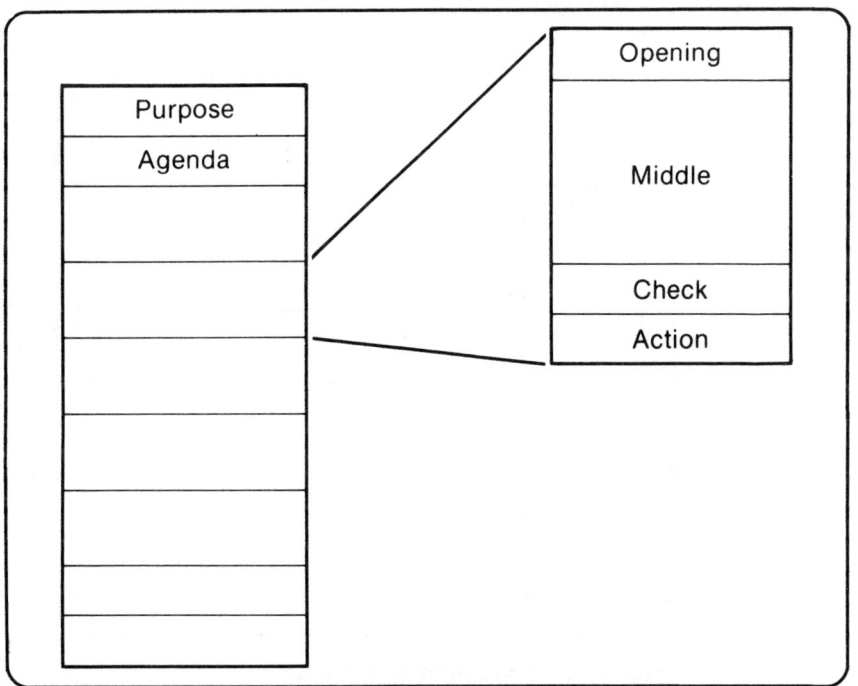

Fig. 4   Components of the middle sections

Remember that each section of the middle also has an opening, middle and ending (see Figure 4): first the introduction of the subject and the reason for discussing it; then the discussion itself; following which the appraiser checks to make quite sure that the information both parties have is correct.

Much of the success depends on the quality of the information that is obtained and shared. This in turn depends on the the way questions are asked (see Chapter 4). The questioning process is shown in Figure 5. It can be likened to a chemical funnel where the raw, crude liquid (information) enters and passes through a series of filters (questions) of increasing fineness until the refined product finally emerges and can be checked and processed.

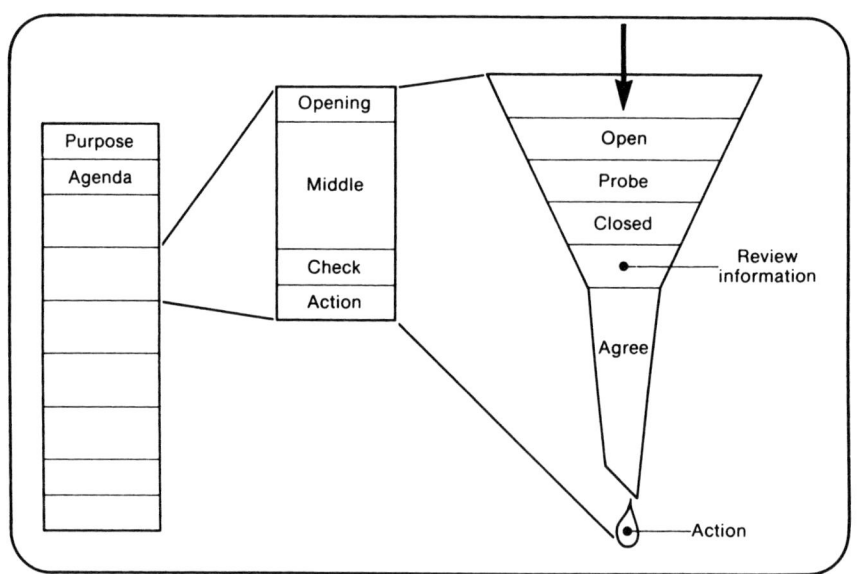

Fig. 5 The questioning process

If the first filter is too fine it can be enlarged by the use of a reflective to increase the flow of information. Finally action needs to be taken, remembering that commitment from the appraisee is likely to be more useful than compliance.

The next section of the tape deals with two agenda items of this interview. Firstly the point that both Harold and John wanted to discuss, that of stock levels with particular reference to John's objectives last year. Following this Harold raises the question of John's relationship with his supervisors.

Start the tape

Harold	Stock levels were top of your list, so let's start with those. I had a rough time from Peter over Sundown – what were your stock levels at the beginning of August?
John	They were about 90% of last year's.
Harold	90%? But you know last year was a bad year and so was the year before. . .
John	Yes, I know, that's why I cut stock levels to 90% . . . there was no way of knowing that orders would be 50% up on last year. . .
Harold	Yes, but surely last year chemists were overstocked from the previous year; did you make allowances for that? John, it mustn't happen again; we must keep stock levels to an adequate level. You'd better get together with Marketing every month and in good time to review offtake against target . . . on reflection, I think I'd better be involved to make quite sure that Peter has no comebacks.
John	Well, all right, if you say so. . .
Narrator	OK. Harold's identified the problem, got the information, given John the solution and he's going off to action it; nothing wrong with that. . . . Or is there?
	Let's listen to that scene again.
Harold	Stock levels were top of your list so let's start with those. . .

Narrator	Good start, but about to be spoilt because his next statement will signal that he is already biased.
Harold	I had a rough time from Peter over Sundown.
Narrator	John's been forced into a position where he has to defend himself, so he puts up the barriers and from now on Harold is unlikely to get all the information that he could have. He further limits it by asking a closed question which invites a single fact in answer.
Harold	What were your stock levels at the beginning of August?
John	They were about 90% of last years'.
Harold	90%? But you know last year was a bad year and so was the year before. . .
John	Yes, I know, that's why I cut stock levels to 90% . . . there was no way of knowing that orders would be 50% up on last year. . .
Harold	Yes, but surely last year chemists were overstocked from the previous year; did you make allowances for that?
Narrator	Harold thinks he has nailed John and has identified the problem to his own satisfaction. He now imposes his own solution.
Harold	John, it mustn't happen again; we must keep stock levels at an adequate level. You'd better get together with Marketing every month and in good time to review offtake against target . . . on reflection I think I'd better be involved to make quite sure that Peter has no comebacks.
John	Well, all right, if you say so. . .
Narrator	Harold has missed the signs of compliance and has probably ensured that John will not try hard to make this solution work. And by involving himself he has virtually said to John that he doesn't trust him to carry it out properly. Also, because Harold didn't check the

information he had, or try to see if John had a point of view, he never found out that the cost-cutting exercise agreed during the previous appraisal was in fact a large part of the cause. In consequence he solved the wrong problem, hence John's lack of commitment.

But thankfully we can all learn from experience and so can Harold.

Harold	John, you mentioned the question of stock levels – tell me about it.	(open question)
John	Well, last year we agreed that I would aim towards reducing stock levels by 5%. By and large that's gone pretty well, almost every line is down by the 5% and in two cases we've been able to reach 10%, but it depends on having accurate offtake targets.	
Harold	And have you?	(probe)
John	Well, no, in the case of Sundown they hopelessly underestimated and I had to do 16 hours overtime on the line to make the target. The point is that I'm doing my damnedest to keep stock levels to a minimum and then getting caned because I'm not meeting orders – they can't have it both ways, Harold.	
Harold	I see – exactly how much were they over target?	(closed question)
John	About 50%.	
Harold	And your stocks?	(closed question)
John	They were about 10% down on the same time last year.	
Harold	Was there any reason for that?	(probe)
John	Yes, there was. Last year they overestimated their offtake and I was left with one hell of a high stock – I wasn't going to get caught the same way twice.	
Harold	John, were there any factors which made last year different from this one?	(Harold knows the answer but wants John to think it through.)
John	Well, I suppose it was a pretty bad summer last year, like the year before, so chemists may have had surplus stocks. . .	

John	Well . . . perhaps because the weather was so good I should have checked with Marketing . . . but they didn't check with me either.	
Harold	So what you are saying is that we need to keep stocks to a minimum but at the same time it's vital that we fulfil orders quickly; right?	(check)
John	Right.	
Harold	So how are we going to solve that one?	(Harold wants John to arrive at his own solution.)
John	Well, it ought to be possible to revise the computer program so that we have tighter control of offtake against stocks to give us more warning of variations.	
	I'll ask Marketing to give us information on trends, that might keep them more on the ball too and take care of the late order situation.	
Harold	Yes, good idea; let's recap. The stock reduction exercise might have contributed; your decision to reduce to 90% certainly did contribute but so did that lot in Marketing by not giving you earlier warning.	(summary)
	I think what you are now suggesting is fine and that should avoid any repetition. Bring me up to date when you've seen Marketing, would you? – end of the month?	(action)
John	Fine, end of the month. I'm sorry if I put you in a spot.	
Harold	In the meantime I'll have a word with Peter Jarvis. I'll give him Sundown.	
Narrator	Quite a difference . . . So how has Harold achieved this result? Well, a good part of his success is related to the types of question he chose to filter the information. First he asked a nice open question.	
Harold	John, you mentioned the question of stock levels – tell me about it.	
Narrator	Then he further clarifies this information by a probing question.	

John	. . . 10%, but it depends on having accurate offtake targets.
Harold	And have you?

Narrator	The probe, followed by a couple of closed questions to get detailed information.

Harold	I see – exactly how much were they over target?
John	About 50%.
Harold	And your stocks?
John	They were about 10% down on the same time last year.
Harold	Was there any reason for that?

Narrator	Probe.

John	Yes, there was. Last year they overestimated their offtake and I was left with one hell of a high stock – I wasn't going to get caught the same way twice.
Harold	John, were there any factors which made last year different from this one?

Narrator	Another probe.

John	Well, I suppose it was a pretty bad summer last year, like the year before, so chemists may have had surplus stocks. . .

Harold	Yes, so. . .

John	Well . . . perhaps because the weather was so good I should have checked with Marketing . . . but they didn't check with me either.

Narrator	Having got what he considers to be almost pure information, Harold checks it.
Harold	So what you are saying is that we need to keep stocks to a minimum, but at the same time it's vital we fulfil orders quickly; right?
John	Right.
Narrator	Now, having got the pure information and had it confirmed, he wants to settle on a course of action – preferably one determined by John himself. In this way he is more certain of John's commitment.
Harold	So how are we going to solve that one?
John	Well, it ought to be possible to revise the computer program so that we have tighter control of offtake against stocks to give us more warning of variations. I'll ask Marketing to give us information on trends, that might keep them more on the ball too and take care of the late order situation.
Harold	Yes, good idea.
Narrator	Positive reinforcement. Now he summarizes the action.
Harold	Let's recap. The stock reduction exercise might have contributed; your decision to reduce to 90% certainly did contribute, but so did that lot in Marketing by not giving you earlier warning. I think what you are now suggesting is fine and that should avoid any repetition. Bring me up to date when you've seen Marketing, would you – end of the month?
John	Fine, end of the month. I'm sorry if I put you in a spot.
Narrator	There is every indication of commitment because John has suggested the

solution himself. We are always more committed to our own plan than to someone else's.

Harold has set a definite time for the action – end of the month. Most importantly, John has learned from the discussion and does not feel punished.

Now let's hear how Harold deals with something even more difficult, that is, the sensitive question of relationships. . .

Harold	. . . so you'll do that? Good.
	Now I want to discuss your relationships with your supervisors, John. They seem to be slipping a bit.
John	What do you mean?
Harold	Well, there seem to be a few rumblings.
John	Such as?
Harold	Nothing specific – just a few veiled hints and so on.
John	What sort of hints?
Harold	Well, Jim Jackson said to me 'We don't seem to be trusted any more'.
John	When was that?
Harold	Oh, the other day when I was around the plant.
John	What does he mean, 'not trusted'?
Harold	It was something about rejections – he said he had to refer everything to you before he could stop the line.
John	That's right, but he doesn't take any notice. He stopped it again this morning and then told me about it afterwards. Anyhow, Jim's got no right to go shooting his mouth off behind my back – there have been far too many rejects for petty little reasons. I'll have this out with Jim; those supervisors are getting far too big for their boots.
Harold	Hold on, John, don't go off the deep end, it was only a casual remark. Just

try to be a bit more tactful in the future, after all you can't risk upsetting those people, can you?

Narrator   If you are going to get involved in this sort of situation make sure you have your facts at hand. Harold was appearing to criticize . . . 'they seem to be slipping a bit'. This caused an immediate defensive reaction. He had no *real* evidence, only gossip which he assumed was fact. A more considered strategy is necessary. . .

Harold   Right then, that's another action sorted out; is there anything else you want to say?

John   No, I'm happy with that.

Harold   So let's move on. . . . I think there's only one more thing before we talk about the future and that's something that does concern me . . . You've got a lot of extra work on your plate now and, OK, you've told me how much you're going to delegate to George, but I wonder about the supervisors – is there anything more we can give to them? (open)

John   Oh, I wouldn't delegate any more to them.

Harold   You wouldn't? Why? (probe)

John   Well . . . I've probably overdone it already . . .

Harold   Overdone it? (reflective)

John   You know I gave them total responsibility for quality? Now it's a problem . . . no, it isn't a quality problem. Look, what's happened is, it's become a quality versus output problem. . . They're driving me to distraction, particularly over the packaging – if the quality isn't absolutely perfect they stop the line to adjust it. If it was really necessary I wouldn't mind, but 90% of the time it isn't; it's got so bad that I've now had to tell them not to stop the line without my approval. Even so, I had to give Jim a rollicking today because he'd stopped the line again – had it stopped for over an hour. I'll

	never meet my production targets unless I keep the line running.	
Harold	John, just a minute – you gave them total responsibility for quality and now you've taken it back – right?	(check)
John	Yes.	
Harold	Why was that?	(probe)
John	It was because they kept stopping the line for insignificant quality faults.	
Harold	But, surely, quality is important?	(reflective probe)
John	Of course, but in this case it was reducing output unnecessarily.	
Harold	And so affecting your targets?	(leading)
John	Yes.	
Harold	So you'e worrying over quality because it's affecting your production targets?	(check)
John	Yes, I suppose so.	
Harold	So how did you communicate that to the supervisors?	(probe)
John	Well, I just told them that it couldn't go on; they were stopping the line too often.	
Harold	What exactly did you say to them?	(probe – Harold wants to find out how John went about it.)
John	Er . . . I said that they were letting minute quality variations interfere too much with production, that it couldn't go on, and they weren't to stop the line without my permission unless there was an obvious fault. . .	
Harold	How did they react to that?	(probe)
John	Well, I suppose they looked a bit shocked.	
Harold	How would you have felt?	(Harold is starting to edge John to a realization.)
John	It was the right thing to do, but I suppose I could probably have done it a bit better.	
Harold	A bit better?	(reflective)
John	Well . . . yes . . . a lot better. Actually it's bothered me a bit.	

Harold	Mmm. So what can we do about it now? . . . They've got their objectives too.	(again, use of 'we' to get John's solution)
John	Yes, of course they have. Maybe I should get them together and explain what the score is?	
Harold	Well . . . What will you say to them?	(Harold wants to check how John will go about it)

John Well, I'll say that I understand their responsibility for quality, but if we don't get these orders out we'll lose them for ever, therefore production is absolutely vital at the moment . . . Maybe I ought to clarify the standards and relate them to. . .

Narrator Harold has now really begun to achieve effective appraisal interviewing skill. If we go back and analyse his technique, what do we find? Firstly, how he introduced the subject and got John to reveal his side of the story.

Harold OK, you've told me how much you're going to delegate to George, but I wonder about the supervisors – is there anything more we can give to them?

John Oh, I wouldn't delegate any more to them.

Harold You wouldn't? Why?

John Well . . . I've probably overdone it already . . .

Harold Overdone it?

John You know I gave them total responsibility for quality? Now it's a problem . . . no, it isn't a quality problem. Look, what's happened is, it's become a quality versus output problem. . . They're driving me to distraction, particularly over the packaging – if the quality isn't absolutely perfect they stop the line to adjust it.

Narrator He now picks up on a crucial piece of information.

John	. . . I'll never meet my production targets unless I keep the line running.
Harold	John, just a minute – you gave them total responsibility for quality and now you've taken it back – right?
John	Yes.
Narrator	Listen to John revealing his own problem as a result of Harold's questioning.
Harold	Why was that?
John	It was because they kept stopping the line for insignificant quality faults.
Harold	But, surely, quality is important?
John	Of course, but in this case it was reducing output unnecessarily.
Harold	And so affecting your targets?
John	Yes.
Harold	So you're worrying over quality because it's affecting your production targets?
John	Yes, I suppose so.
Harold	So how did you communicate that to the supervisors?
John	Well, I just told them that it couldn't go on; they were stopping the line too often.
Harold	What exactly did you say to them?
John	Er . . . I said that they were letting minute quality variations interfere too much with production, that it couldn't go on, and they weren't to stop the line without my permission unless there was an obvious fault. . .
Harold	How did they react to that?
John	Well, I suppose they looked a bit shocked.
Harold	How would you have felt?
John	It was the right thing to do, but I suppose I could have probably done it a bit better.

Harold	A bit better?
John	Well . . . yes . . . a lot better. Actually, it's bothered me a bit.
Harold	Mmm. So what can we do about it now? . . . They've got their objectives too.
John	Yes, of course they have. Maybe I should get them together and explain what the score is?
Harold	Well . . . What will you say to them?
John	Well, I'll say that I understand their responsibility for quality, but if we don't get these orders out we'll lose them for ever, therefore production is absolutely vital at the moment . . . Maybe I ought to clarify the standards and relate them to. . .
Narrator	This is the second time that Harold has gone through the whole range of useful questions: open question, probe, reflective and closed. Then he checks and considers the information, finally producing clear and concise action.

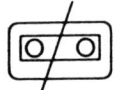 *Stop the tape and return to the text.*

Dealing with the future

In the preceding scenes Harold has cleared the ground for discussing John's future. This is a difficult subject for an appraiser, as very often you have little direct influence.

However, it is of vital concern to the appraisee and you must remember that you are often the only link the appraisee has with the organization's promotion network.

It is very easy to dodge this problem by being vague or, even worse, 'dangling a carrot'. If the appraisee's expectations are raised and later not fulfilled, severe demotivation will result. Vague replies will be frustrating. The aim should be to be as realistic and *constructive* as possible.

In the next scene we shall hear Harold's way of dealing with this problem.

 *Start the tape*

Harold	Now, I promised to come back to the subject of your future.
John	Ah yes. . . Well, I've done five years in this job now and I think that I'm ready for some more responsibility . . . like a bigger job. I'm also getting to the point where in order to keep George motivated I've had to delegate quite a lot of what I do . . . So I'm getting quite concerned about what my next move is – it's not that I'm unhappy in the job – just a feeling that I could make a bigger contribution, and I also know that Steve Wilson is retiring in Southampton, so I wonder if I could be considered for that. I think it's time to make the next step, I reckon I've earned it and I could always do with the money . . . and I've had good assessments for the last two or three years.
Harold	Yes, you have, you've performed well in your present job. Have I got this straight – you obviously want to progress; and you see progression as more of a sideways move into a bigger, but similar job, rather than directly upward, and you feel that you have the capacity to do it?
John	Yes, that's about right, but of course I wouldn't mind moving upwards. . .
Harold	OK. I understand all that. Remember that there are specialists in the company on career development and if you like I can arrange for you to talk to them. If you do go for it you

	are going to have to produce some evidence that you can do it. I know that you are doing this job well, but let's see what evidence we can produce to show that you have the capacity to do a bigger job. Have you had any thoughts about it?
John	Well, no, not really.
Harold	So let's look at what you've done over the last few years. . . *(Fade)*
John	I think you're right, Harold, I would like a bit more time to think about it. Can you give me a month?
Harold	Yes, sure. John . . . What's going to happen if after all this you don't get a bigger job? How's it going to affect you?
John	Of course I'd like a promotion, and if I don't get it I'm not the only one who's going to be disappointed, but I hope it won't alter things between us?
Harold	No, John, of course it won't. Personally I'd be sorry to see you go, but for your sake I'd be delighted.
Narrator	In that scene Harold first listened and then checked. He got John to redirect his thinking and he checked whether he had fallen into the trap of thinking that because he was doing his present job successfully it automatically meant he could do a larger job equally well. Being able to juggle three plates doesn't mean you can juggle four. He checked the very important question of what would happen if John *did not* get promotion. It is all too easy to raise expectations and store up trouble if they are not realized.

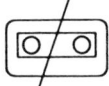 *Stop the tape and return to the text.*

In this chapter we have laid great stress on the correct use of questions and the effect that this has on the quality of the information obtained. In the same way, if appraisers reveal their own values, they are bound to influence their appraisees' replies. Obviously this skill is not confined to the appraisal situation and is equally important in dealing with day-to-day situations where accurate information is an essential part of the decision making process.

It is a skill that can be constantly practised either in conversation or in operational situations – all it requires is an awareness of the process that is taking place.

The table shows the various situations where different types of questions or statements are of use or otherwise.

Question/statement	Useful	Not useful
OPEN 'Tell me about. . .' Encourages the appraisee to talk.	In most openings. To explore and gather information.	With talkative appraisee. Where discipline is required.
PROBING 'Exactly what happened next?' Vital for detail; 'open' question to clarify what appraisee means.	To check information.	To explore emotionally charged areas.
CLOSED 'How old were you then?' Narrow; establishes specific points of fact.	To obtain single facts.	To gain information in areas not normally explored by appraisee.
REFLECTIVE 'You feel upset about the move.' Very powerful. Repeat back verbatim the emotional content of an appraisee's statement.	In problem-solving. In emotionally charged situations. In counselling.	To check information or fact.

LEADING 'I suppose you're sorry now, are you?' Invariably leads to answer you expect.	To gain acceptance of your view.	To gain any information about appraisee.
HYPOTHETICAL 'What would you do if . . . ?' Posing a hypothetical situation in the future.	To get appraisee to think about new areas.	With appraisee who needs time to give a reasoned reply.
MULTIPLE String of questions/statements.	Never.	Always.
NON-COMMITTAL 'Yees', 'Aha', 'Mmmm'. Lubricates the discussion.	To get the appraisee to expand his views.	To keep a garrulous appraisee to the point.
COMPARISON 'Would you prefer to advance on the managerial or the technical side?'	To get the appraisee to explore and reveal his own needs, values, etc.	Where 'pairs' are unrealistic or irrelevant.
SUMMARIES 'What we seem to have decided so far is that . . .' Draws together main points of discussion.	To ensure that details are not forgotten. To gain commitment to plan of action.	When premature.

8 The ending

Endings are all-important. There is no need to end lamely, and the closing minutes can be used to:

- make quite sure that there is nothing else the appraisee wants to talk about. *Then*

- summarize actions agreed (or imposed).
- reinforce success.
- where appropriate, leave the employee confident of the future.
- make sure the appraisee knows exactly what to do and why.

It often pays to have the appraisee do much of the talking because:

1 Getting the appraisee to summarize what actions each side has undertaken makes sure that they both have the same understanding.
2 Appraisers can watch for signs of compliance in issues where they think they have the appraisee's commitment. In such a case it may be worth re-opening the issue to find out why the appraisee's mind has changed.

The process is illustrated in Figure 6.
In summary endings should answer:
- What have we agreed?
- What are you going to do?
- What am I going to do?
If there is doubt – *re-open the discussion!*

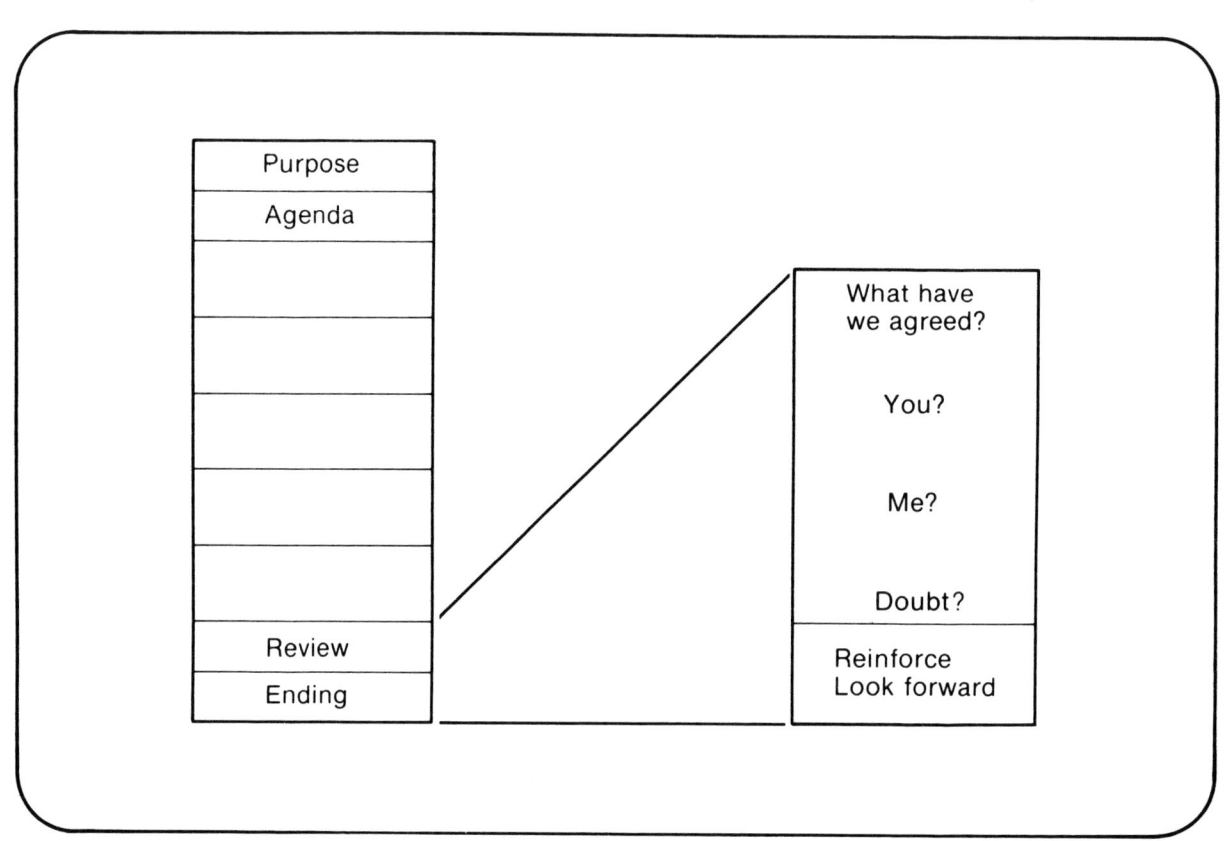

Fig. 6   The ending

Harold	Well, I hope we've dealt with everything you wanted to discuss. Is there anything else which has occurred to you while we've been talking?
John	No, I don't think so.
Harold	Let's recap on what we've agreed. First, you're going to do two things with regard to that stock level problem: you're going to have a look at the computer program to tighten the control of offtake against stocks; and also you're going to see Marketing to ask them to give you earlier trend information – and that's by the end of the month.
John	Yes. OK.
Harold	Next, we agreed that you would . . . *(Fade)* . . . and that should help to clear that. Next, you're going to discuss with your supervisors this production versus quality issue – with the emphasis on 'discuss', please, John.
John	OK, Harold, I'll do it, don't worry.
Harold	And finally, your future . . . You said you'd like a month to think about it.
John	Yes, I'm going to need the time.
Harold	OK. I'll draft out the appraisal form and let you have it in a couple of days. You know, John, when all's said and done, we make a good team – let's keep it up, shall we? That's it, not a bad appraisal, was it?

Narrator	Well, was it? John gave a powerful signal which Harold ignored. Harold doesn't know that John is not totally committed to one of the courses of action previously agreed.
	     If Harold had made John do the summary he would then have heard John's understanding of the agreed actions and his level of commitment – remember, it's the last chance to check the success of the review.
	     Let's hear it done that way. . .

Harold	Well, I hope we've dealt with everything you wanted to discuss. Is there anything that's occurred to you while we've been talking?
John	No, I don't think so.
Harold	Right, so perhaps you'd like to recap on what we've agreed.
John	First, I'm going to do two things with regard to that stock level problem: I'm going to have a look at the computer program to tighten the control of offtake against stocks; and I'm also going to see Marketing to ask them to give me earlier trend information.
Harold	By when?
John	The end of the month. I'm also going to . . . and that should help to clear that. Next, I've got to talk to the supervisors.
	And finally, bearing in mind the way you encouraged me to look at my performance, I'd like to think it over again before discussing it with Career Development in a month's time . . . I think that's it.
Harold	John, you rather skipped over that quality problem.
John	I said I'll do it, Harold.
Harold	You don't sound too happy with it.
John	Look, Harold – it's this question of standards. According to the written specifications on the packaging they are absolutely right to stop the line and if I tell them that they will just dig their heels in and continue as before.
Harold	When we talked it through, we agreed that you had to meet the production targets because otherwise we would lose orders. But I also understood that you were going to tell them the whole problem and try and get them to solve it.
John	Yes, I am, but I don't want it to go on longer than is necessary. The sooner we get the new packaging the better.
Harold	Do you want me to lean on them?
John	If you can shorten the delivery down to two weeks then I should be able to persuade the supervisors to relax their standards until then.
Harold	Great, are you happy with that now?
John	Yes, fine.

Harold   OK, that's it, I'll draft out the appraisal form and let you have it in a couple of days. You know, John, when all's said and done it's not been a bad year, has it?

Narrator   Well, Harold finally seems to have developed a good technique for appraisal interviewing.

There's nothing magic about it, but it's not that easy either. It does require preparation, it does require awareness, it does require skill, but above all it needs you to remember that your aim is to help your subordinates get better at their jobs.

Doing it this way turns appraisal into an active, constructive and skilful conversation between two people.

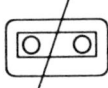 *Stop the tape and return to the text.*

Monitoring and reporting

However successful the interview, the appraisal process obviously does not end there. Harold said to John that he would *draft* out the form and let him have it in a couple of days – implying that it could still be changed if necessary. However, if he does the job properly the appraisal form should not surprises John when he sees it, nor should the performance rating or salary increase that he is subsequently awarded. We have deliberately said nothing about this aspect. What matters is that any appraisal system should be seen by employees to be fair, and a manifestation of fairness is that there should be no surprises as a result of the interview.

It is all too easy to leave it there – to return the form to the personnel department and forget about it until the next time. If this happens, credibility will suffer and, with it, employees' commitment to appraisal. Monitoring the actions agreed is a vital component and must not be neglected, particularly where the employee's development and training are concerned.

Conclusion

We stressed at the outset that there is no one right way to carry out an appraisal interview. The important thing is that your strategy and your style are appropriate to that appraisee at that time.

What we have tried to do is to show that, whatever your approach, the acquisition of skill is the key. There is no substitute for formal training in developing skill, but a structure on the lines we have illustrated, together with an awareness of the process, will lay a firm foundation for development. Your skill will be enhanced by:

- Careful preparation with a clear idea of the purpose.
- Getting the opening right – the purpose and the agenda – what it's about and what you both want to talk about.
- Using the appropriate questions and style in the middle – the agenda points.
- Ending each agenda point with a firm commitment to action. By this means success will build on success.
- Ending the interview by checking whether both of you know what has been agreed and ending on a high note.
- Being analytical about your own performance and the process that is taking place. Ask yourself 'what is the *next step* I should be taking to become a better interviewer?'
  Finally, the appraisal process can be summarized by asking:

- What did you ask of him/her?
- What *did* he/she do?
- Why is this?
- What are you *both* doing about it?

Appraisal is not just a management tool for guiding the strengths and weaknesses of your staff. It also helps you discover your own, and in so doing increases the effectiveness of your company's management as a whole.

Appendix 1: Behaviour patterns of management styles

Style can be identified by the actions of the interviewer and the responses he encourages or accepts from the subordinate. The four basic behaviour patterns in identifying style are:

Authoritarian: Values held by the interviewer are paramount in judging the subordinate. He tells the subordinate how he should behave differently and shows approval of compliance and conformity. He states the subordinate's problems, the solution and details the actions he must take to improve. Little or no input from the subordinate.

Benevolent: The appraiser's own values and experience are significant in judging the subordinate. He reveals the subordinate's problems by relating his behaviour to its effects. Appraiser then sells solutions. Some input from subordinate.

Consultative: The appraiser judges the subordinate's behaviour in terms of its effects upon performance. Brings out performance points in open, value-free discussion, will listen and offer solutions, sometimes choosing his own solution in preference to that offered by subordinate. Fair input by subordinate.

Participative: The appraiser and the subordinate jointly explore behaviour in terms of its effects upon performance. Brings out problems encountered by the subordinate in open, value-free discussion and helps him to his own solutions, accepted by the manager. Substantial input by subordinate.

Figure 7 shows another way of demonstrating the effect of style – a model designed by Tannenbaum and Schmidt. The hatched sector shows the degree of authority exerted by the manager, leaving the white sector as freedom of action by the subordinate. At each end of the continuum there is always a small amount of freedom left.

The real skill lies in selecting the right place on the continuum for a given situation, and the skilful manager will move up or down the continuum as and when the situation demands.

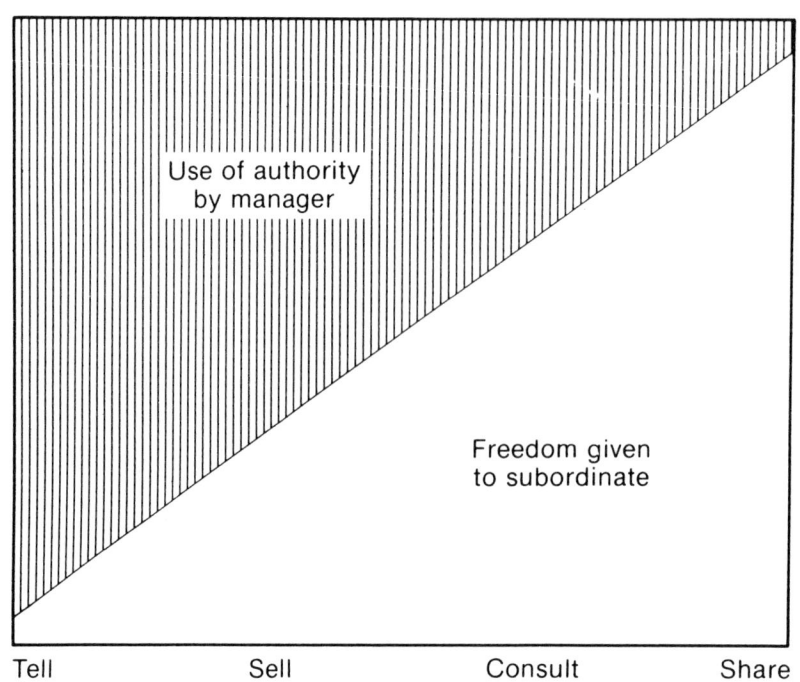

Fig. 7   The Tannenbaum and Schmidt leadership continuum

Appendix 2: Further reading

Gill, D., *Appraising performance: Present trends and the next decade*, Institute of Personnel Management, 1977.

Mager, R.F. and Pipe, P., *Analysing performance problems*, Pitman, 1970.

Randell G.R., 'Management Education and Training' in W.T. Singleton, *Management Skills*, MTP Press, 1981.

Randell, G.R., Packard, P.M.A. and Slater, A.J., *Staff Appraisal – A first step to effective leadership*, Institute of Personnel Management, 1984.

Singer, E.J., *Effective Management Coaching*, IPM, 1971.

Stewart, V. and Stewart, A., *Practical Performance Appraisal*, Gower, 1977.

Wright, P.L. and Taylor, D.S., *Improving Leadership Performance*, Prentice-Hall, 1984.